This journal belongs to

....

Ellie Claire
Hachette Book Group
1290 Avenue of the Americas, New York, NY 10104
ellieclaire.com

First edition: September 2019

Ellie Claire is a division of Hachette Book Group, Inc. The Ellie Claire name and logo are trademarks of Hachette Book Group, Inc.

The publisher is not responsible for websites (or their content) that are not owned by the publisher.

Print book interior design by Bart Dawson.

ISBN: 9781546014423 (hardcover)

Printed in China
RRD-S
10 9 8 7 6 5 4 3 2 1

Introduction

When something is exceptional, it means that it stands out from the crowd, is extraordinary, and is something to be celebrated. You are God's masterpiece, formed in His image and created to do great things.

Along with the book *Exceptional You!*, this journal is meant to help you discover or uncover the very best of who you are and to become the extraordinary person God created you to be. Each page contains important thoughts from the book that serve as daily reminders of how exceptional you truly are. Contemplate these thoughts as you write about your daily life, and be encouraged to make each day count.

Let this be a record of your daily progress and your entries a testimony to your growing faith. You are fearfully and wonderfully made. Embrace that truth and see life as more than mundane and ordinary—live exceptionally!

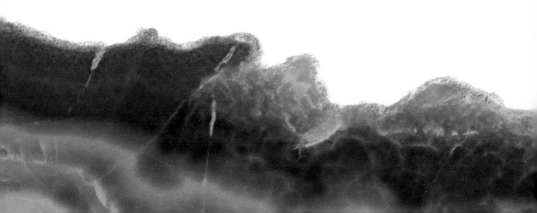

God is by your side. He is always offering us a new beginning and a fresh start.

God has each of us on a path. No two are the same. But the destination God has for all of us is victory. When you are faithful with what God has placed in your hand, and you don't allow it to become mundane and ordinary, you are living exceptionally.

We all face challenges and unfair situations, but if we are willing to take steps of faith and place them in God's hands, that's when the exceptional in us is produced.

efore the foundation of the world, it pleased God to adopt you
as His very own child. He looked through the corridors of time
and knew you by name. He handpicked you and brought you
into His family through Jesus Christ.

Get up every day and remind yourself that the Creator of the universe chose you and you are valuable to Him.

....

....

....

....

....

....

....

....

....

....

....

....

....

....

....

....

....

....

....

....

....

....

Even before he made the world, God loved us and chose us
in Christ to be holy and without fault in his eyes.
God decided in advance to adopt us into his own family.

EPHESIANS 1:4–5 NLT

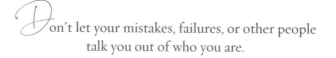

*Don't let your mistakes, failures, or other people
talk you out of who you are.*

....

....

....

....

....

....

....

....

....

....

....

....

....

....

....

....

....

....

....

....

....

....

....

Quit beating yourself up for things you can't change.
God wants you to move forward in faith, believing that you are chosen,
exceptional, and well able to do what He has called you to do.

God had already chosen David to be king of Israel long before he was tending his father's sheep out in the fields.... His family might have counted him out, but God had already counted him in.

. . . .

*G*od knew what was on the inside of David. God also knows
what's on the inside of you, because He put it there.
He knows what you're capable of.

If we are going to accomplish our dreams and reach the fullness of our destiny, we must press past our excuses and put aside the no, grab hold of our yes, and take bold steps of faith.

It is up to me to unpack

what God has already lovingly placed

inside me for my special assignments.

I will work with God to develop

and bring forth the life

He has planned for me.

*N*othing has the
power to change
God's plan for
your life.

$\mathcal{H}$old your head up high and put your shoulders back. Scripture says you are a "royal priesthood" and "God's special possession" (1 Peter 2:9 NIV)....
Adjust your crown and wear it like you know who you are.

You are royal priests, a holy nation, God's very own possession. As a result, you can show others the goodness of God.

1 PETER 2:9 NLT

God does not want us to doubt our worth and abilities.
Don't go through life from a position of lack when
God has made you more than enough. You have the qualities you need
to have successful relationships, a good career, and a strong family.
You have the right gifts, the right talents, and the right personality.

We have to push past fears, mistakes, and excuses
in order to develop what God has placed in us.

Your faith may feel as if it's being tested and pushed to the extreme. Remember, it's the trial of your faith that brings out the lasting character in your life and builds confidence you cannot attain any other way.

The only difference between a piece of black coal and a precious diamond is the pressure it has endured.

....

....

....

....

....

....

....

....

....

....

....

....

....

....

....

....

....

....

....

....

The pressure you may be facing isn't going to break you—
it's going to make you. It's going to develop you and give you
experiences you need to build your confidence. Honor God
and believe you have what it takes to shine brightly for Him.

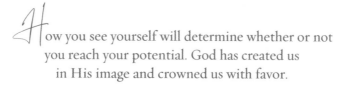

How you see yourself will determine whether or not
you reach your potential. God has created us
in His image and crowned us with favor.

....
....
....
....
....
....
....
....
....
....
....
....
....
....
....
....
....
....
....
....
....

We all face disappointments, we all make mistakes, but that's not who we are.

God is saying the same thing to us today that He said to Moses: Go, and I will help you. Go, and I will teach you.

Who has made man's mouth?... Have not I, the LORD?
Now therefore, go, and I will be with your mouth
and teach you what you shall say.

EXODUS 4:11–12 NKJV

If there is a yes in your heart, it is because God placed it there. It's time to act on your yes.

$\mathcal{G}$od has an assignment with your name on it. It is an assignment
He wants you to accomplish for Him.

Jesus said, "I am the vine; you are the branches" (John 15:5 NIV).
When you stay connected to Christ, you are connected
to the power source.... With God, you can move past those limited
mind-sets that are trying to hold you back and walk through
those doors of opportunity that God has opened for you.

I can break bad habits.

I can have good relationships.

I can forgive.

I can be successful.

I can overcome.

I can do all things through Christ.

*Y*ou may feel like the odds are against you, but what God has promised will come to pass. It's not going to come through other people; it's going to come through you.

....

....

....

....

....

....

....

....

....

....

....

....

....

....

....

....

....

....

....

....

....

Fan into flames the spiritual gift God gave you.

2 TIMOTHY 1:6 NLT

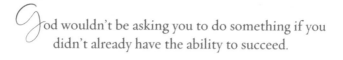

God wouldn't be asking you to do something if you
didn't already have the ability to succeed.

Trust that God is in control, that He's not only directing your steps,
but also directing the steps of the people you need.

When we put on that winning attitude, it will shift the way we approach even the most challenging situations.

When you choose to see through your eyes of faith, not fear,
you will come out of the wilderness moments stronger
and more determined than you were before.

God wants to build confidence in us so we can have faith that He will always be there for us.

$\bigcup$e won't always see every step of the way, but He shows us enough
to comfort, encourage, and empower us to move forward.

It's never too late to get back in line with God.
You can still become everything that He created you to be.

....
....
....
....
....
....
....
....
....
....
....
....
....
....
....
....
....
....
....
....
....

God's mercies are new every day. If you fall down, you don't have to stay down. You can get back up because of the mercy and the grace of Almighty God.

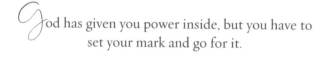

God has given you power inside, but you have to
set your mark and go for it.

Set your minds on things above, not on earthly things.

COLOSSIANS 3:2 NIV

It is time for you to rise and shine. Lift your eyes and look beyond this problem at the new opportunities that [God has] in your future.

Everywhere we go, God has put a banner of victory over our heads.
It signifies this truth: "I am a child of the Most High God.
I am destined to live in victory. I can do all things through Christ.
When the enemy comes against me, I will raise my banner of victory."

We don't have
to wait for our
difficult situations
to be resolved
before God will
do a new thing.
He is always at
work in our lives.

Forget the former things; do not dwell on the past.
See, I am doing a new thing! Now it springs up; do you not perceive it?
I am making a way in the wilderness and streams in the wasteland.

ISAIAH 43:18–19 NIV

Every morning when you get out of bed, put that flag of victory over your head. Remind yourself who you are. Align yourself with God.

God, I may be in a difficult season but that doesn't stop You from working in my life. In the meantime I'm going to fly my flag of victory; I'm going to go through this day in faith, grateful, being a blessing wherever I go.

Imitate those who through faith and patience inherit the promises.

HEBREWS 6:12 NKJV

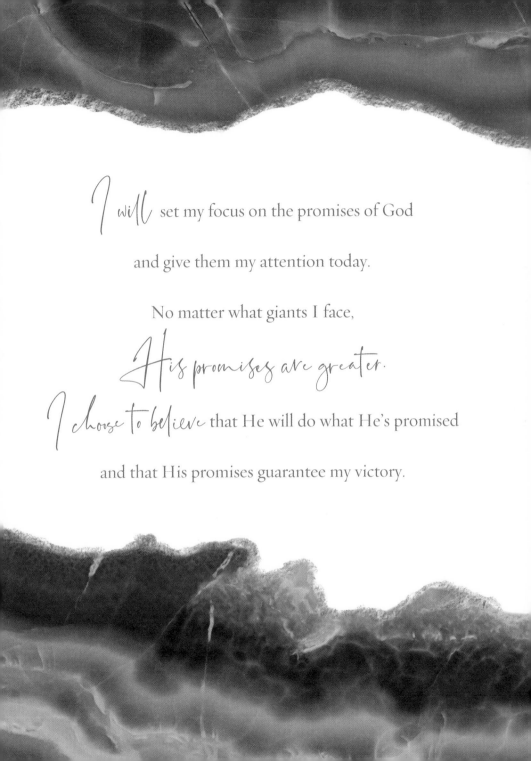

I will set my focus on the promises of God

and give them my attention today.

No matter what giants I face,

His promises are greater.

I choose to believe that He will do what He's promised

and that His promises guarantee my victory.

$\mathcal{H}$e is our source. He knows what we need. If we are going to be
our best and live exceptional, we need to get in a habit
of spending time with God every day.

....

....

....

....

....

....

....

....

....

....

....

....

....

....

....

....

....

....

....

....

....

I pray that out of his glorious riches he may strengthen you
with power through his Spirit in your inner being,
so that Christ may dwell in your hearts.

EPHESIANS 3:16–17 NIV

Keep your heart with all diligence, for out of it spring the issues of life.

PROVERBS 4:23 NKJV

*E*very day you have the choice to either
store up the good or accumulate the bad.
Be aware of what is taking root in your heart.

We must be committed to keeping our memory box so full of good treasure there is no room for the negative.

Remembering the right things will strengthen your faith and help you overcome your difficulties.

When you remember what God promised you, it keeps you encouraged, it builds your faith, and it helps you move forward and become exceptional.

*E*very one of us has seen God's goodness and favor.
He's made ways where it didn't seem possible.... We can't let
what was once miraculous become something ordinary.

Scripture says that David remembered how he had killed a lion and a bear with his own hands (see 1 Samuel 17:37). What gave him strength was remembering his past victories and how God helped him overcome.

....

....

....

....

....

....

....

....

....

....

....

....

....

....

....

....

....

....

....

$\mathcal{I}$f you're going to stay encouraged...you have to remember that lion and bear you killed in the past, those victories when God helped you overcome what you could not face on your own.
Those are your memorial stones....Write them down and read them out loud. Tell them to your family and children.

If you're going to be exceptional, you must learn to encourage yourself. Get up every day and begin to declare who God says you are. "I am a child of the Most High God. I am loved by God. I am strengthened by God. I am accepted by God and I am full of purpose and destiny."

As you continue to encourage yourself, you will have the ability
to see the best not only in yourself, but also in others.

We have to remind ourselves that we are not failures; we are learners....
We are all in the process of becoming who God created us to be.
It is up to us to stay encouraged along the way.

Maybe you feel as if you have fallen down today, but let me assure you
that God is a good Father and He is cheering you on.
He is supporting you along the way.

When you resist the temptation to speak negative words, you will direct your life out of the rough waters and set your course for victory.

*D*avid prayed, "Set a guard over my mouth, LORD;
keep watch over the door of my lips" (Psalm 141:3 NIV)....
He knew the power of his words.

*I*t's time to
let the doors of
disappointment
close behind you
so you can step
forward into the
new things God
has in store.

God will take what the enemy meant for harm, and use it to your advantage. Reach forward to those things that are ahead of you and take your swing. That's where your success lies.

*J*esus said, "[My words] are spirit and they are life" (John 6:63 NKJV)....
Take the words of God and speak them audibly out of your mouth. It will
change your thoughts and lead you to your miracle.

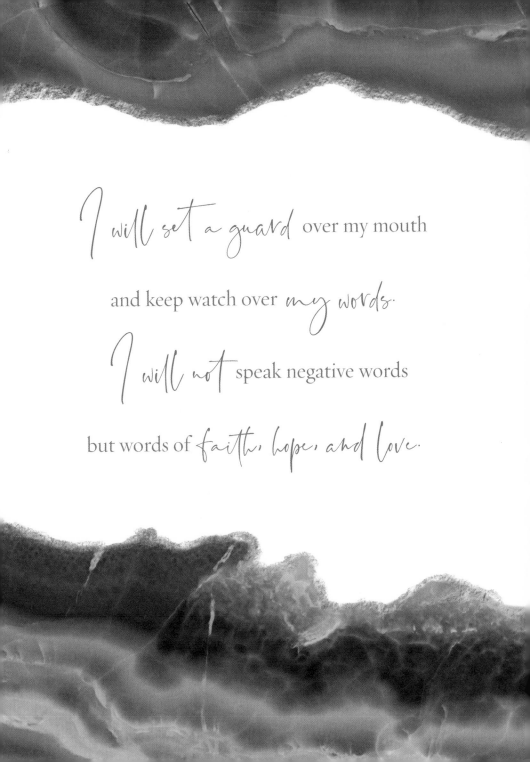

I will set a guard over my mouth

and keep watch over my words.

I will not speak negative words

but words of faith, hope, and love.

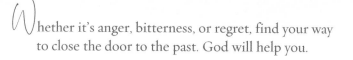

Whether it's anger, bitterness, or regret, find your way
to close the door to the past. God will help you.

God's Word works when you put it into your heart and mind.

Don't keep looking back. God has a new and better plan....
Yesterday's mistakes stay in your yesterday. Good things are
in your future. Believe it, take hold of it, and watch it come to pass.

....

....

....

....

....

....

....

....

....

....

....

....

....

....

....

....

....

....

....

....

*S*tart the day in faith, casting your worries on the Lord,
trusting that He's guiding and directing your steps.

For I know the plans I have for you," declares the LORD, "plans to prosper you and not to harm you, plans to give you hope and a future."

JEREMIAH 29:11 NIV

Make the choice to walk through the process of recovery. Fill your mind and heart with messages of hope from God's Word. It will build courage and determination and fill you with faith and victory.

Don't worry about anything; instead, pray about everything. Tell God what you need, and thank him for all he has done.

PHILIPPIANS 4:6 NLT

....

....

....

....

....

....

....

....

....

....

....

....

....

....

....

....

....

....

....

....

....

God knows that there will be times we feel overwhelmed.
Paul didn't just say, "Don't worry."
He told us how to win the war on worry. He said,
"Pray about everything" (Philippians 4:6 NLT).

When you welcome Him into the middle of your challenges, you'll have strength that you didn't have, peace when you could be upset, and faith to enjoy each moment.

....

....

....

....

....

....

....

....

....

....

....

....

....

....

....

....

....

....

....

....

Talk to God about everything that concerns you.
That's what prayer is. He wants to help us through life,
but He's waiting for us to come to Him.

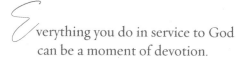

*Everything you do in service to God
can be a moment of devotion.*

$\mathcal{G}$od means for you to find joy in your work, joy with your kids in the house, and joy doing the dishes as well as watching the movie that follows.... He wants us to live each moment of our lives as if we were still sitting at His feet, like Mary.

*I*t takes the same amount of energy to worry as it does to believe.

When you put your everyday tasks into the hands of God, and use them to honor Him, you make every day, and every moment, exceptional.

Don't miss today by worrying about tomorrow. If what concerns you does come to pass, you can be assured it's not a surprise to God. He'll give you the grace to handle it.

$\mathcal{W}$orry is not only strangling your joy and peace,
it limits what God will do. When you believe, angels go to work;
when you believe, negative situations will turn around;
when you believe, dreams come to pass.

*L*ive this day in faith, trusting that God's in control. He knows what you need.

$\mathcal{W}$hat is the price of two sparrows—one copper coin?
But not a single sparrow can fall to the ground
without your Father knowing it.

MATTHEW 10:29 NLT

Write down Scripture verses that are filled with the promises of God and what He says about you. Place them where you will see them every day as a physical reminder and a memorial stone of God's truths.

....

....

....

....

....

....

....

....

....

....

....

....

....

....

....

....

....

....

....

I will start a memory box today, of things

people have said, compliments they have given,

words that remind me of *who I am*

as a child of the Most High God.

I will return to that box whenever I need

to feed my *confidence* and *joy* and offset

negative thoughts that are playing in my mind.

Get up each morning and make the declaration, "Today is going to be a good day." When you put this into practice, you'll live the exceptional life that belongs to you.

We hold the power to lift each other up, every day,
to remind each other of the goodness of God.

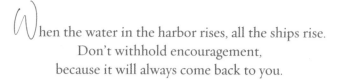

When the water in the harbor rises, all the ships rise.
Don't withhold encouragement,
because it will always come back to you.

A generous person will prosper;
whoever refreshes others will be refreshed.

PROVERBS 11:25 NIV

When we speak encouragement to others, we not only breathe God's love into them, but we also breathe God's love into our own soul.

$\mathcal{W}$e want to help our loved ones feel like winners, because that is
what they are. We are called to encourage them,
cheer them on, and build them up.

We are better together. God has ordained people in your life for you to strengthen as well as people to strengthen you. None of us have gotten where we are by ourselves.

Over thirty times in Scripture we find the phrase *one another*....
Encourage one another. Serve one another.
Comfort one another. You need "one anothers" around you.

*S*omeone needs your encouragement.
Someone needs to know that you believe in them
and you believe that they can succeed.

A hug, a handshake, a high five, these are simple gestures
that can take on healing properties that can encourage
and bind us together in love.

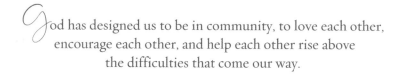

God has designed us to be in community, to love each other, encourage each other, and help each other rise above the difficulties that come our way.

$\mathcal{B}$e an encourager each and every day and watch your community grow strong, tall, and able to withstand any attack from the enemy.

*Y*ou do not need to perform great acts of service. God wants us
to be on the lookout for little ways that we can do good.

When you read about the life of Jesus, time and time again it says
that when He saw people in need, He was *moved* with compassion.
He didn't just feel pity; His compassion led to action....
We are called to do the same.

There's a reason you feel compassion for people. It's not an accident. It's God sending you a message of how you can do His work.

To be exceptional, we understand that to love well, we have to feel compassion and allow it to move us into helpful action.

We are called
to follow love
and let it guide
us to right action.
Compassion is
from God and
it has miracle
working power
in it.

This is the commandment, as you have heard from the beginning,
that you continue to walk in love [guided by it and following it].

2 JOHN 6 (AMPC)

For us to be exceptional, God wants us to be people who are willing to open our hearts of compassion and follow God's divine flow of love.

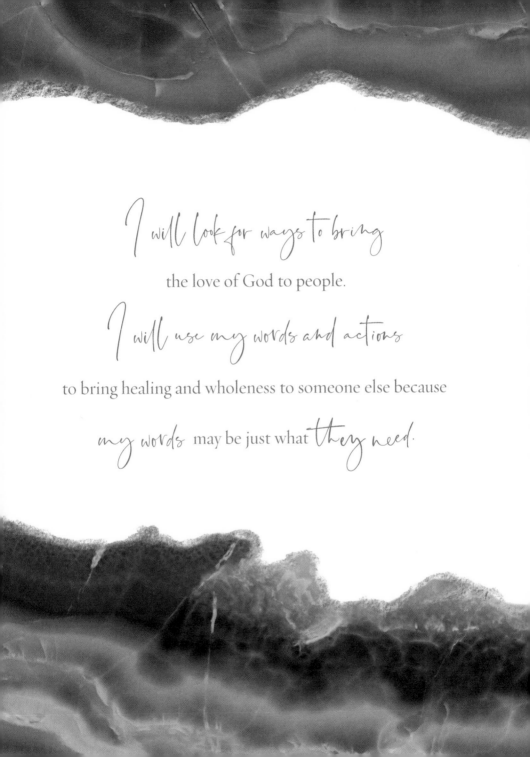

I will look for ways to bring

the love of God to people.

I will use my words and actions

to bring healing and wholeness to someone else because

my words may be just what they need.

Those feelings you get for other people are messages from God.
He wants you to reach out. He wants you to act.
He wants you to love.

Be quick to recognize that divine flow of love wherever it leads.
Don't put it off.

When you value your spouse, your children, you don't throw words
around that you don't mean.... You realize they're not ordinary;
they're not common. They are precious, gifts from God.

God works where there's an attitude of faith.
Be grateful and stay at peace.
No matter what comes against you, find the good.

As we have opportunity, let us do good to all people.

GALATIANS 6:10 NIV

To be exceptional means you understand God's call on your life.
Love well. Don't miss any opportunity to be a blessing,

The happiest people are those who appreciate the blessings in their lives and don't underestimate their value.

....

....

....

....

....

....

....

....

....

....

....

....

....

....

....

....

....

....

....

....

....

....

....

Look closely at the people God's placed in your life, and rediscover
the virtue, the value, and the beauty in them.

When you see through the eyes of a grateful heart,
you will appreciate all the beauty that lies around you.

Life is fragile. Find reasons to be grateful.
They are always there if you look for them.

I will look for ways to bring an attitude of gratitude
into all aspects of my life. And to practice
being grateful in the good times and bad.

*I*t is amazing how God knows what is best for us.

Trust God's timing. Yes, pray for God's hand to be guiding you, be excited about the future, but remember that in the waiting there is a preparation that is taking place.

When we learn to wait well, we will strengthen our muscle of patience and that's when we will see the promise come to pass.

*P*atience means
you know that you
can trust God no
matter how long
it takes. It's the
key ingredient
to waiting well.

Those who wait for the Lord [who expect, look for, and hope in Him]
shall change and renew their strength and power;
they shall lift their wings and mount up [close to God] as eagles...;
they shall run and not be weary.

ISAIAH 40:31 AMPC

Waiting with expectancy is waiting actively. You are praying, believing, and preparing for it to happen.

*L*ike the farmer, you've planted. You've prayed. You've watered your seed.
You've thanked God. You can have the confidence that says,
"Not *if* it happens but *when* it happens."

God is always at work in our lives. Even during the wait, He is active. He is nurturing and strengthening and preparing and encouraging.

We will renew our strength when we are *actively* waiting on God.
Preparing ourselves in the wait. Knowing that this season
is preparing us for the next.

God wants us to have goals, He wants us to dream big,
but we have to trust His timing.

Just like winter gives way to spring, the wait will give way
to the good things of God.

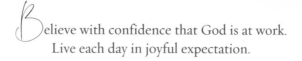

Believe with confidence that God is at work.
Live each day in joyful expectation.

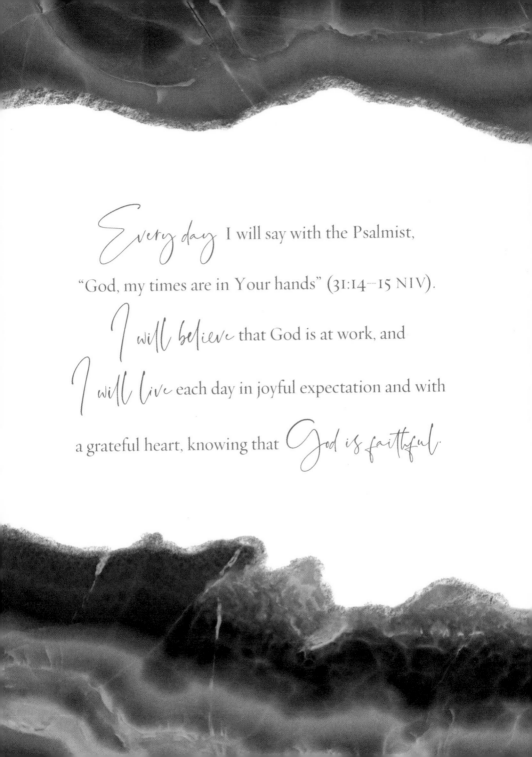

Every day I will say with the Psalmist,

"God, my times are in Your hands" (31:14–15 NIV).

I will believe that God is at work, and

I will live each day in joyful expectation and with

a grateful heart, knowing that God is faithful.

To live your exceptional life, come close to Him so you can be reminded who you really are, His beloved child.

But God demonstrates his own love for us in this:
While we were still sinners, Christ died for us.

ROMANS 5:8 NIV

Our faults, mistakes, and wrongdoings don't drive Him away; they draw Him closer.

There's nothing on the inside of you that would make you distant from God. In Jesus, you are made right with God. He loves you just the way you are and He came to you just the way you are.

The LORD is close to the brokenhearted and saves
those who are crushed in spirit.

PSALM 34:18 NIV

The Bible says: He knew you before the foundation of the world.
He chose you in His great love for you. He says you are
His precious treasure. He even counts every single hair on your head.

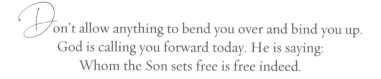

*D*on't allow anything to bend you over and bind you up.
God is calling you forward today. He is saying:
Whom the Son sets free is free indeed.

....
....
....
....
....
....
....
....
....
....
....
....
....
....
....
....
....
....
....
....

Sometimes God's mercy shows up when we don't feel like
we have any more strength to believe.

*N*ever lose sight of the fact that the Creator of the universe is closely watching you.

Don't give up, keep believing, keep praying.
You may be ready to give up on a dream but God isn't.
He still has a way to bring it to pass.

See, I have engraved you on the palms of my hands.

ISAIAH 49:16 NIV

$\mathcal{B}$efore we check in with the world, we should check in with God. We should fuel ourselves with His Word, His promises, and His proclamations, and then we'll enter each day with more power.

The right thoughts are empowering. They will cause you to rise above discouragement and limited mind-sets that would try to hold you back.

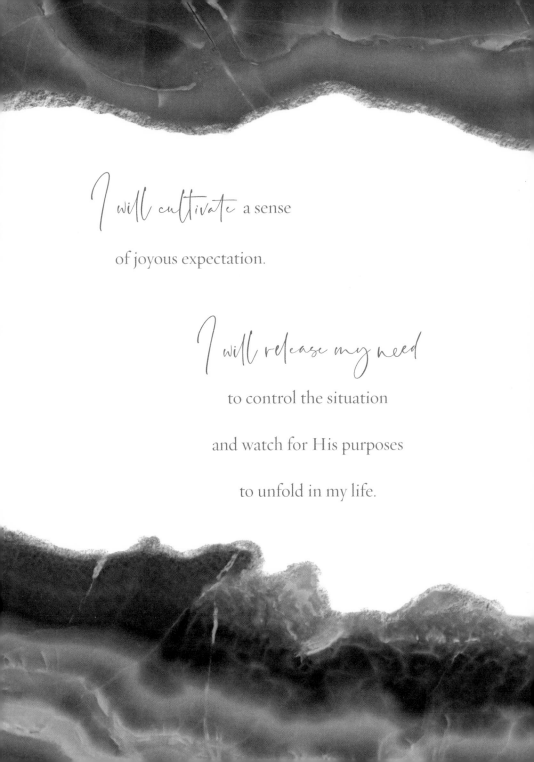

I will cultivate a sense

of joyous expectation.

I will release my need

to control the situation

and watch for His purposes

to unfold in my life.

Just like our physical body gets refreshed and reenergized
when we sleep at night, we need to take time
to strengthen and fuel our inner man.

God wants you to be strong and have self-control
so you can rise higher and go farther.

When we pay attention to this core of who we are, we can move into each day with strength.

Reading the Scriptures is nourishing your inner man with spiritual food.
Being quiet and thanking God for His goodness is spiritual food.
Declaring God's promises over your life feeds the core of who you are.

You have to set aside time with God as a vital part of your life.

God is waiting for us to draw near to Him, to call out to Him each day. Scripture says to call out to God and He will show you great and mighty things.

Every day get up and thank God for your health, your relationships,
your family, and your job. By starting your day this way,
your inner man is being nourished.

You will seek Me, inquire for, and require Me [as a vital necessity]
and find Me when you search for Me with all your heart.

JEREMIAH 29:13 AMPC

*J*esus said: I am the bread of life. I am the living water.
If you drink of Me you'll never thirst again.
Are you drinking from the living water?

_____

_____

_____

_____

_____

_____

_____

_____

_____

_____

_____

_____

_____

_____

_____

_____

_____

_____

_____

*D*uring the day when things come against us, it's stressful, and you have opportunities to get upset. Take a five-minute break to gather your thoughts and reach out to God.... Pray in your heart, "God, I need Your help. Thank You for Your peace. I'm asking for Your strength." When you do that, you just took a drink.

*G*et up each morning and connect to the power source by spending time with God. Draw strength from Him. Receive His wisdom.... If you'll do this, you'll come up higher and higher. God will pour out His blessings and favor and you'll live the exceptional life He has in store for you.